The Bear Said Please
Written and Illustrated by Jacque Duffy
Published by Wombat Books, 2014
Second Publication by Itchy Emu Publishing, 2023

2nd Edition

The illustrations in this book are watercolour painted on Saunders Waterford 300gsm paper.

National Library of Australia Cataloguing-in-Publication entry
Author:      Jacque Duffy
Title:       The Bear Said Please / Jacque Duffy
ISBN:        978-0-6450313-9-3 (pbk)
Target audience: Pre school, Primary School
Subject:     Manners

Itchy Emu Publishing

To all the little kids in my life,
especially Bentley and Aston.

"Growl," said the bear.

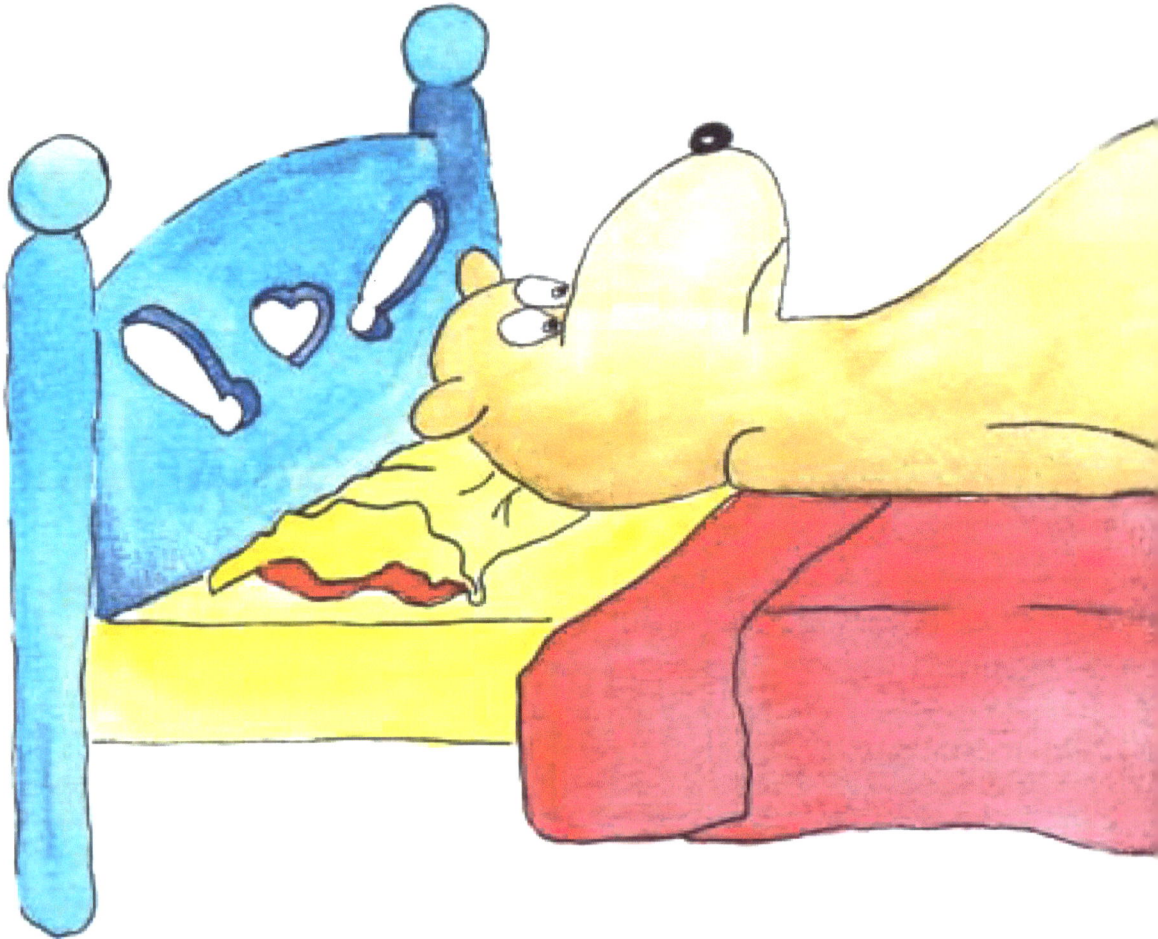

"Growl," said his tummy.

"Hmmmm,"
thought the bear.

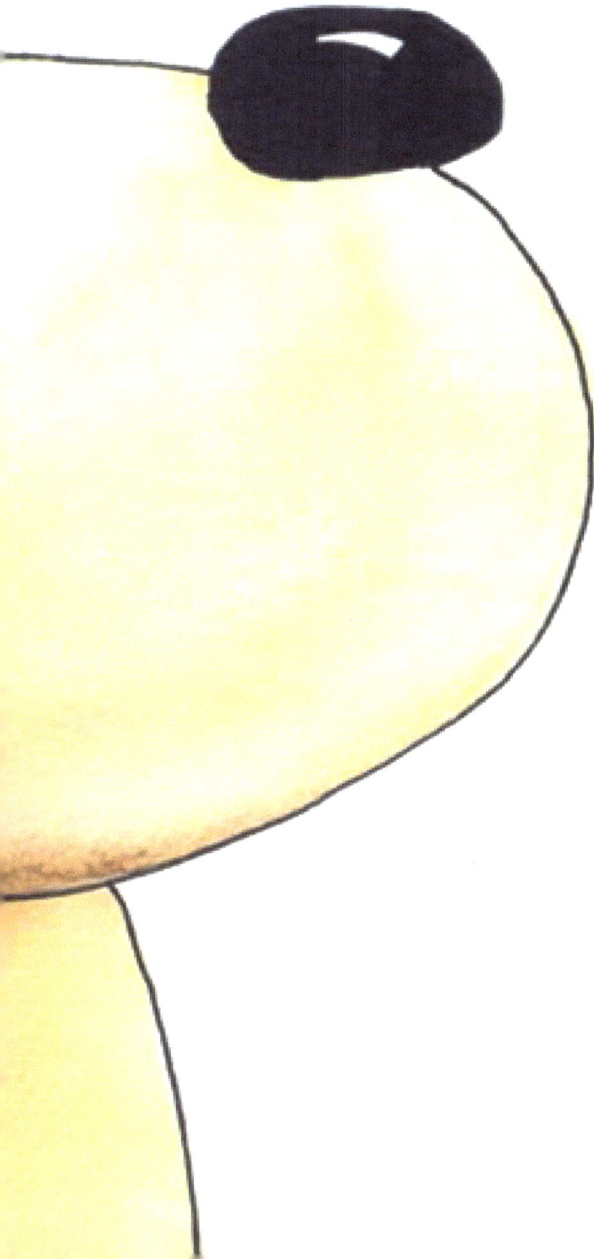

"I need some honey."

The bear looked up.

The bear looked down.

The bear looked all around............

"Hmmmm," said the bear.

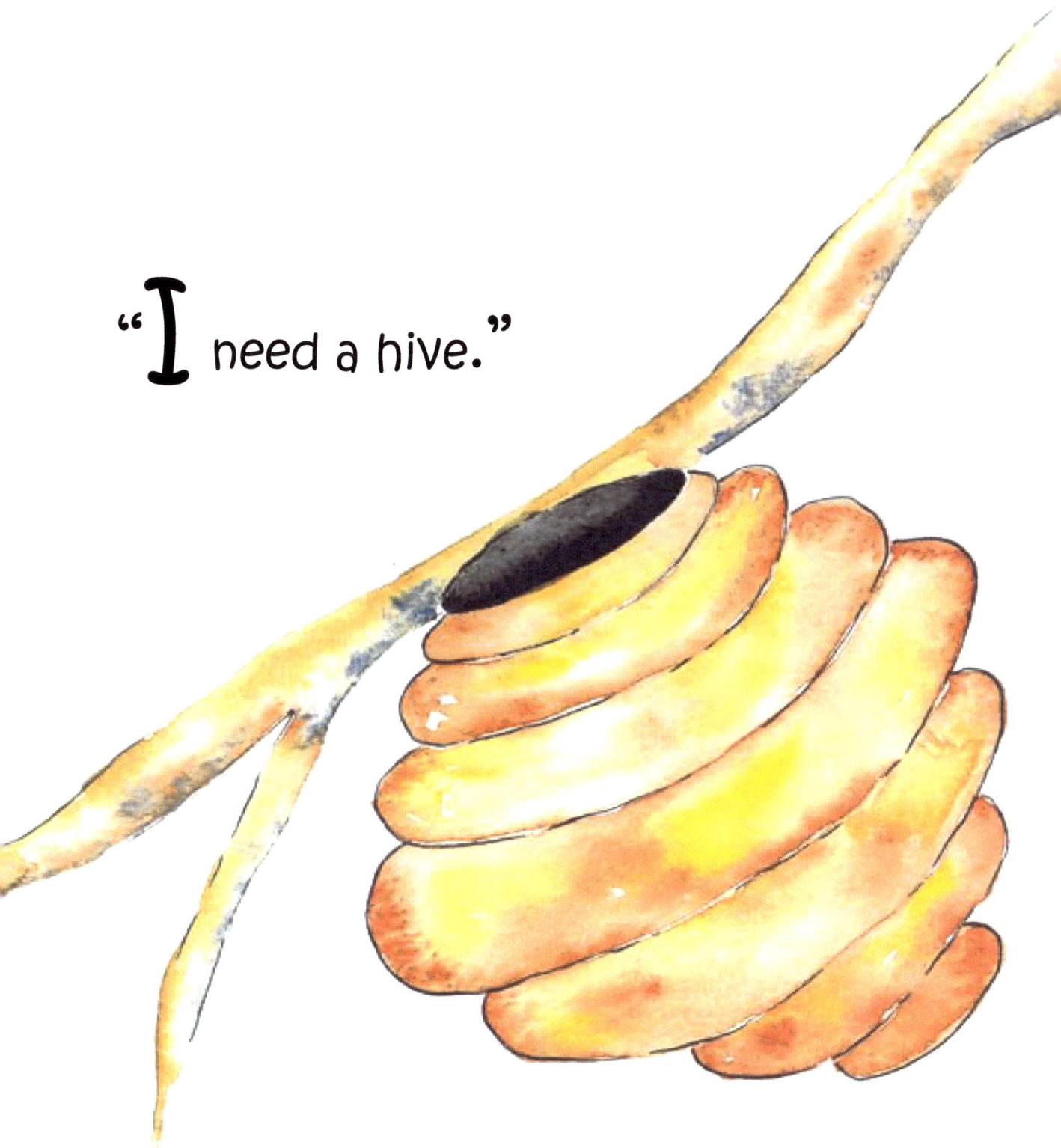

"I need a hive."

He hopped in his car,

and went for a drive.

He went into the forest....

# Into the trees.

# There he found
some busy bees.

Up went the bear...

$H$e
climbed
to
the
top.

**W**hen
he reached
the hive
he had to
stop.

The bees were angry.
The bees were mad.

# Not saying

# PLEASE

## is very

# BAD!

"Ouch!"
cried the
bear.

And without much grace, the bear

fell down, landing on his face.

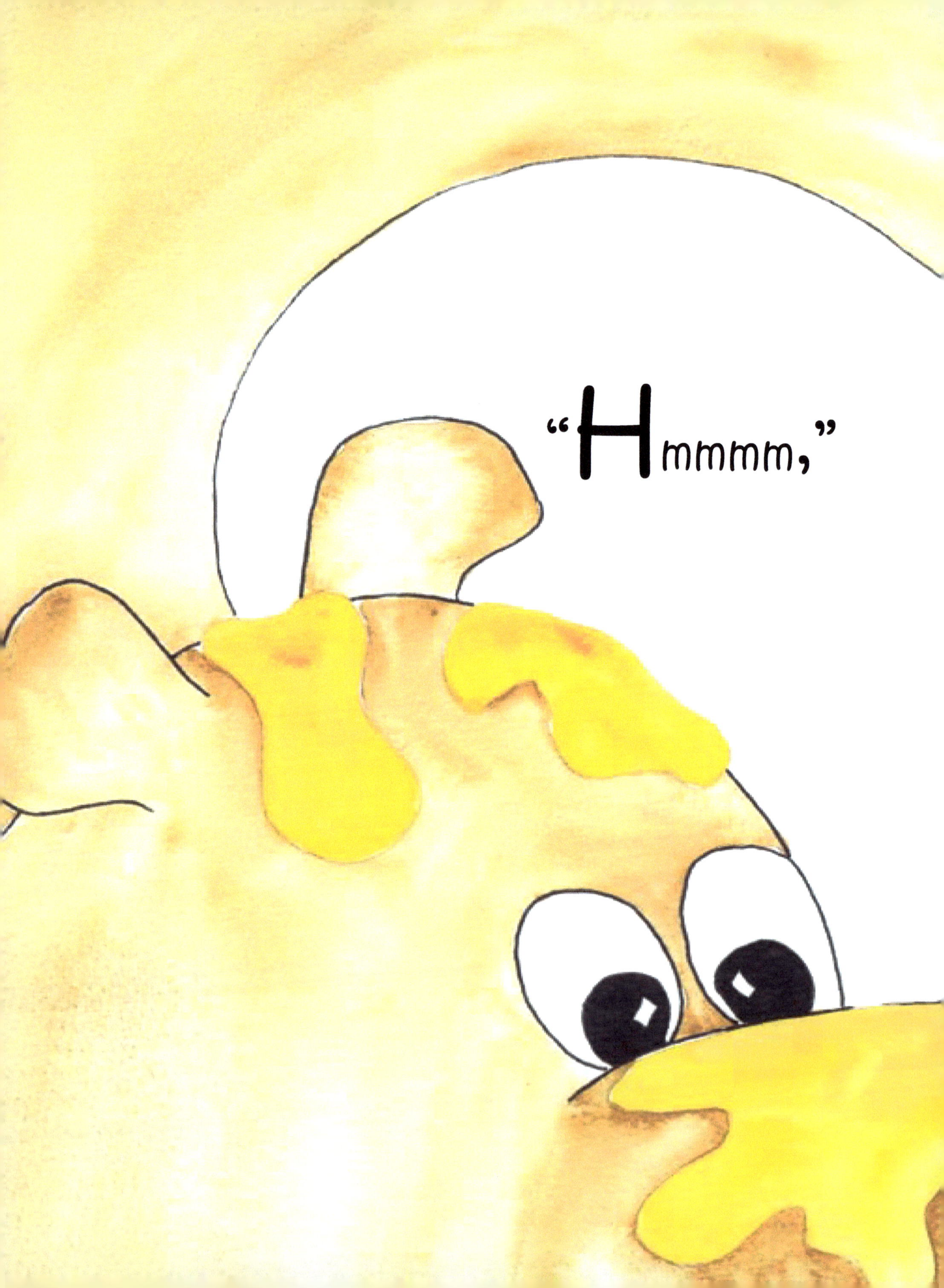

"Hmmmm,"

thought the bear as he licked

honey from his paw.

"I should use my
manners more!"

"Sorry," said the bear, as he gave

flowers to the bees.

"May I

have some honey

please?"

The bees said

"YES,"

the bear was polite,
they gave him

HONEY,

with great delight.

(Then the bear said...  "Thank you very much!")